Boogie Dog and Guinea

Melinda Bramlett Joyner

This book is dedicated
with love to my grandchildren:

Weller, Emilee, Max, Sarah, Oliver, Austin, Bram
and Jack; and to my niece Katie

To order additional copies of this book, contact:
Xlibris
844-714-8691
www.Xlibris.com
Orders@Xlibris.com

Illustrated by: Jan Michael Vincent Sy

ISBN: Softcover   978-1-4568-6765-2
             EBook   978-1-5434-9962-9

Print information available on the last page

Rev. date: 09/20/2021

He spent the days romping,
as most puppies do,

Digging up flowers and
chewing on shoes.

As new homes were found for
all puppies but him,

The chance of a new home was
now growing dim.

This pup as he grew just would not stay home;

He chewed through the fence so at will he could roam.

Then a wonderful
family who lived
in the hills

Played with the
puppy and saw
his strong will.

5

He ran like the wind, and could not be caught,

So they took him to stay, to train him, they thought.

6

That day this puppy that was
almost full grown

Had a home in the mountains
where he was not alone.

They all called him "Boogie"; this name matched his speed;

At last he could run with no fences to heed.

Boogie was happy; he romped all day long

With Bud, George, and Little Joe, he was growing up strong.

These dogs and the cats, oh,
their hearts he did win;

But who would have
thought a wild bird would
move in?

This wild bird, a guinea, just showed up one day.

She looked the place over and decided to stay.

The animals all left this
Guinea alone,

But Boogie knew how it felt
to be new to a home.

When dinnertime came, and the dogs all took theirs,

Boogie moved from his dog-dish, with Guinea he'd share.

13

So while all the others would eat and go play,

Boogie waited for Guinea; he did this each day.

As spring turned
to summer, young
Guinea remained

With her new
brother, Boogie,
she romped and
she played.

When down the road, running,
Boogie would stride,

With wings flapping, running,
Guinea stayed by his side.

16

Curled up next to Boogie
at night you would see

A big sleeping Guinea as
content as could be.

To see this red hound dog, his
bed he would lend,

Who would have thought
Boogie would be such a friend?

Some mornings when all the
dogs ran off and stayed,

Guinea stood on the hill
calling Boogie to play.

19

So down from the mountain,
as fast as he could,

He'd run back to Guinea; she
knew that he would.

So now this red hound dog, so lanky and tall,

Was known far and wide as the one Guinea would call.

He lives with his family; they know he is clever,

But to Guinea, this wild bird, he's her brother forever.

Printed in the United States
by Baker & Taylor Publisher Services